Mother Angelica *Tour* *Prayer Book*

MotherAngelicaTour.com

Compiled by: Barbara A. Gaskell

Photography by: Christopher Cugini

Cover art by: Tracy Dawn Brewer

Canton, Ohio | 2019

Copyright © 2019 Barbara A. Gaskell

All rights reserved. This book or any portion thereof may not be reproduced or used in any manner whatsoever without the express written permission of the publisher except for the use of brief quotations in a book review.

Printed in the United States of America

First printing 2019

ISBN 978-1-7336090-0-5 paperbound

Library of Congress Control Number: 2019902019

Cover Art by Tracy Dawn Brewer

Design and photography by Christopher Cugini

St. Raphael Center, Inc.
4365 Fulton Dr. N.W.
Canton OH 44718

www.straphaelcenter.com

This book is dedicated to
Suzanne M. Houseman
February 6, 1944 – June 27, 2018
May she rest in peace.

"A faithful friend is a sure shelter,
whoever finds one has found a rare treasure."
- Sirach 6:14

Acknowledgements

Thanks to all who have helped in the compilation of this prayer book: Christopher Cugini who not only supplied the photography but also prepared the layout and design work, Rev. Thomas Kraszewski, pastor of St. Anthony Catholic Church, Rev. John Sheridan, pastor of St. Peter Catholic Church, Mother Gertrude and the Poor Clare Sisters of Perpetual Adoration of the Sancta Clara Monastery, and Karen Sigler, Director of the Rhoda Wise Shrine. Thanks to Marni Bennell for proofreading, Betty DeMarco, Tony Agnesi and Sandy Dowding for your continued encouragement and support during the process.

Special thanks to all of "Team Angelica" who have devoted countless hours to launching, sustaining and growing the Mother Angelica Tour. God bless you for your unselfish love of Mother Angelica and the work we do to honor her memory.

Proceeds from this book will be given to the Mother Angelica Tour and St. Raphael Center, Inc.

Table of Contents

Basic prayers..1

Prayer of St. Anthony................................8

The Angelus..9

Spiritual Communion................................14

Holy Spirit...15

St. Thérèse...17

Stations of the Cross................................29

Sorrowful Mother......................................59

Franciscan Prayer......................................65

Liturgy of the Hours.................................71

Rosary..77

Blessed Sacrament....................................79

Litany of Humility....................................89

Divine Child...93

Prayers for the Dead................................97

Rita A. Rizzo was born April 20, 1923. She was baptized September 11, 1923 at St. Anthony Catholic Church in Canton Ohio. She began her spiritual journey with water and the words, "I baptize you…"

Sign of the Cross

In the name of the Father, and of the Son and of the Holy Spirit.

As a child Rita learned her basic prayers:

Our Father

Our Father, Who art in Heaven, hallowed be Thy name; Thy Kingdom come, Thy will be done on earth as it is in Heaven. Give us this day our daily bread; and forgive us our trespasses as we forgive those who trespass against us; and lead us not into temptation, but deliver us from evil.

Amen.

The Hail Mary

Hail Mary full of Grace, the Lord is with thee. Blessed are thou among women and blessed is the fruit of thy womb, Jesus. Holy Mary Mother of God, pray for us sinners now and at the hour of our death.

Amen.

Glory Be

Glory be to the Father and to the Son and to the Holy Spirit. As it was in the beginning, is now, and ever shall be, world without end.

Amen.

Guardian Angel Prayer:

Angel of God, my guardian dear, to whom God's love commits me here. Ever this day be at my side, to light and guard, to rule and guide.

Amen.

Grace before meals

Bless us, O Lord, and these Thy gifts, which we are about to receive from Thy bounty, through Christ our Lord.

Amen.

Gratitude after meals

We give Thee thanks, Almighty God, for all Thy benefits, Who lives and reigns for ever and ever.

Amen.

Apostles Creed

I believe in God, the Father almighty, Creator of heaven and earth,

and in Jesus Christ, His only Son, our Lord, Who was conceived by the power of the Holy Spirit, born of the Virgin Mary, suffered under Pontius Pilate, was crucified, died, and was buried;

He descended into hell;

on the third day He rose again from the dead.

He ascended into heaven, and is seated at the right hand of God the Father almighty; from there He will come to judge the living and the dead.

I believe in the Holy Spirit, the holy catholic Church, the communion of saints, the forgiveness of sins, the resurrection of the body, and life everlasting.

Amen.

Act of Faith

O my God, I firmly believe that You are one God in three divine Persons, Father, Son, and Holy Spirit. I believe that your divine Son became man and died for our sins, and that He will come to judge the living and the dead. I believe these and all the truths which the holy Catholic Church teaches because You have revealed them, Who can neither deceive nor be deceived.

Amen.

Act of Hope

O my God, relying on Your infinite mercy and promises, I hope to obtain pardon of my sins, the help of Your grace, and life everlasting, through the merits of Jesus Christ, my Lord and Redeemer.

Amen.

Act of Love

O my God, I love You above all things with my whole heart and soul because You are all good and worthy of all my love. I love my neighbor as myself for the love of You. I forgive all who have injured me and I ask pardon of those whom I have injured.

Amen.

Morning Offering

O Jesus, through the Immaculate Heart of Mary, I offer You my prayers, works, joys, and sufferings of this day for all the intentions of Your Sacred Heart, in union with the holy sacrifice of the Mass throughout the world, in thanksgiving for Your favors, in reparation for my sins, for the intentions of all my relatives and friends, and in particular for the intentions of the Holy Father.

Amen.

St. Anthony Catholic Church,
Mother's home parish in Canton, Ohio

Rita Rizzo grew up in an Italian parish that had great devotion to their patron, St. Anthony of Padua.

Prayer to St. Anthony

O holy St. Anthony, gentlest of saints, your love for God and charity for His creatures, made you worthy, when on earth, to possess miraculous powers. Encouraged by this thought, I implore you to obtain for me (request). O gentle and loving St. Anthony, whose heart was ever full of human sympathy, whisper my petition into the ears of the sweet Infant Jesus, who loved to be folded in your arms; and the gratitude of my heart will ever be yours.

Amen.

In the years of Rita Rizzo's childhood it was customary for Catholic churches to ring their bells at 6am, noon and 6pm, reminding the faithful to pray the following prayer commemorating the Incarnation of Jesus Christ.

St. Anthony of Padua mosaic,
St. Anthony Catholic Church in Canton, Ohio

The Angelus

V. The Angel of the Lord declared unto Mary,
R. And she conceived of the Holy Spirit.

Hail Mary, etc...

V. Behold the handmaid of the Lord.
R. Be it done unto me according to your word.

Hail Mary, etc...

V. And the Word was made flesh,   (genuflect or strike your breast)
R. And dwelt among us.

Hail Mary, etc...

V. Pray for us, O holy Mother of God,
R. That we may be made worthy of the promises of Christ.

Let us pray:

ALL: Pour forth, we beseech You, O Lord,
Your Grace into our hearts;
that we to whom the incarnation of Christ,
Your Son was made known by the message of an angel,
may by His passion and cross be brought to the glory of His Resurrection. Through the same Christ, our Lord.

Amen.

*Stained glass window at
St. Peter Catholic Church in Canton, Ohio*

ST. MICHAEL THE ARCHANGEL

It was the general practice of the Catholic Church during the years that Rita Rizzo was a youngster, that immediately after Mass, which was said in Latin, the entire congregation recited the prayer of St. Michael the Archangel.

St. Michael Prayer

St. Michael the Archangel, defend us in battle; be our protection against the wickedness and snares of the devil. May God rebuke him we humbly pray; and do thou, O Prince of the Heavenly Host, by the power of God, cast into hell Satan and all evil spirits who prowl about the world seeking the ruin of souls.

Amen.

St. Michael stained glass window,
St. Anthony Catholic Church in Canton, Ohio

Rita Rizzo made her First Communion on June 1, 1930. Several days before her First Communion she received the Sacrament of Confession.

Rite of Confession

"Bless me, Father for I have sinned. (make the Sign of the Cross) It has been (amount of time) since my last confession."

Confess your sins. Listen to what the priest gives you as a penance. Make an Act of Contrition. He will then bless you and absolve you of your sins. Do your penance.

Act of Contrition

O my God, I am heartily sorry for having offended You and I detest all my sins because I dread the loss of heaven and the pains of hell, but most of all because they offend You, my God, Who are all good and deserving of all my love. I firmly resolve, with the help of Your grace, to confess my sins, to do penance and to amend my life.

Amen.

Communion Prayer

O Lord I am not worthy that You should enter under my roof but only say the word and my soul shall be healed.

Spiritual Communion

My Jesus, I believe that You are present in the Most Holy Sacrament.

I love You above all things, and I desire to receive You into my soul.

Since I cannot at this moment receive You sacramentally, come at least spiritually into my heart.

I embrace You as if You were already there and unite myself wholly to You.

Never permit me to be separated from You.

Amen.

Rita Rizzo received her Confirmation on April 7, 1932, from Bishop Schrembs of the Diocese of Cleveland and took the name Frances.

Holy Spirit Prayer

Come Holy Spirit, fill the hearts of Your faithful and kindle in them the fire of Your love.

V. Send forth Your Spirit, and they shall be created.

R. And You shall renew the face of the earth.

Let us pray. O God, Who by the light of the Holy Spirit, did instruct the hearts of the faithful, grant that by the same Holy Spirit we may be truly wise and ever rejoice in His consolations, through Christ our Lord,

Amen.

Secret of Sanctity Prayer

O Holy Spirit, beloved of my soul, I adore You.

Enlighten, guide, strengthen and console me.

Tell me what I should do; give me Your orders.

I promise to submit myself to all that You desire of me and to accept all that You permit to happen to me.

Let me only know Your will.

Amen.

Rita Rizzo began to suffer severe stomach spasms during her teen years. The doctors attempted to help her but nothing worked. After several years of pain and the loss of twenty pounds, Rita visited Rhoda Wise, a local mystic who encouraged her to pray to St. Thérèse of Lisieux asking for her intercession to be cured. Rita said the prayer for nine days and on the ninth day she was completely healed!

Prayer to St. Thérèse

May the Servant of God Rhoda Wise pray this prayer with me.

O beautiful Rose of Carmel, Saint Thérèse of the Infant Jesus, deign according to your promise to descend from Heaven to visit those who implore you, to pour down in profusion those Celestial Graces that are symbolized by the shower of roses that Jesus, your Spouse, has put at your disposal.

Your power is great with His Heart. He can only listen and hear your prayer. I have recourse to you then, O Saint Thérèse of the Child Jesus; assist me in this need (mention your intention.) Speak for me to Jesus and to Mary and obtain for me the grace to live a holy life and die a happy death.

Amen.

Our Father, Hail Mary, and Glory be for the intentions of Rhoda Wise.

Find out more at www.rhodawise.com

St. Thérèse of Lisieux stained glass window, St. Peter Catholic Church in Canton, Ohio

After her healing, Rita Rizzo began to volunteer her time at the Rhoda Wise home. Mrs. Wise was a wife, mother, mystic and stigmatist. She suffered the visible stigmata on First Fridays. This was a great influence on young Rita, who developed a deep appreciation for the passion of Christ.

Prayer before the Crucifix

Look down upon me, good and gentle Jesus, while before Thy face I humbly kneel, and with burning soul I pray and beseech Thee to fix deep in my heart lively sentiments of faith, hope and charity, true contrition for my sins, and a firm purpose of amendment; while I contemplate with great love and tender pity Thy five wounds, pondering over them within me, having in mind the words which David Thy prophet said of Thee, my Jesus: "They have pierced my hands and my feet; they have numbered all my bones."

Crucifix, St. Anthony Catholic Church Canton, Ohio

After Rita was healed she was a changed person. "After my healing all I wanted to do was give my life to Jesus."(Mother Angelica: The Remarkable Story of a Nun, Her Nerve, and a Network of Miracles by Raymond Arroyo, 2007)

Sweet Sacrament Divine

Jesus, my Lord, my God, my all! How can I love Thee as I ought? And how revere this wondrous gift, So far surpassing hope or thought?

Refrain:
Sweet Sacrament, we Thee adore! Oh, make us love Thee more and more. Oh, make us love Thee more and more.

Had I but Mary's sinless heart With which to love Thee, dearest King, Oh, with what ever fervent praise, Thy goodness, Jesus, would I sing! **Refrain**

Thy Body, Soul and Godhead, all! O mystery of love divine! I cannot compass all I have, For all Thou hast and art is mine! **Refrain**

Sound, then, His praises higher still, And come, ye angels, to our aid; For this is God, the very God Who hath both men and angels made! **Refrain**

Crown of Thorns Prayer

Dear Lord, I am grieved when I consider Your sad condition when You wore the Crown of Thorns upon Your Holy Head.

I desire to withdraw the thorns by offering to the Eternal Father the merits of Your Wounds for the salvation of sinners.

I wish to unite my actions to the merits of Your Most Holy Crown, so that they may gain many merits, as You have promised.

Amen.

As Rita deepened her relationship with Jesus, she set up an altar in her bedroom to mimic the altar in the bedroom of Rhoda Wise. On the altar was a statue of the Sacred Heart of Jesus, the Immaculate Heart of Mary and the Infant of Prague. Rita would rise in the wee hours of the morning, kneeling at her wooden prie-dieu offering prayers to the good God that healed her.

Prayer to the Sacred Heart

O most holy Heart of Jesus, fountain of every blessing, I adore You, I love You and will a lively sorrow for my sins. I offer You this poor heart of mine. Make me humble, patient, pure, and wholly obedient to Your will.

Grant, good Jesus, that I may live in You and for You. Protect me in the midst of danger; comfort me in my afflictions; give me health of body, assistance in my temporal needs, Your blessings on all that I do, and the grace of a holy death.

Within Your heart I place my every care. In every need let me come to You with humble trust saying, Heart of Jesus, help me.

Sacred Heart of Jesus statue,
St. Peter Catholic Church in Canton, Ohio

Prayer to the Immaculate Heart of Mary

Glorious Virgin Mary, I long to love your Son, Jesus, the way He deserves to be loved—with the love of your Immaculate Heart.

Unite me to your Immaculate Heart so that I will be open to receive your Son with the same disposition by which you received Him. Your Immaculate Heart is supremely gentle, steadfast, watchful, completely given over to the will of God.

Lead me out of the darkness of ignorance, free me from all selfishness and willful self-assertion, and train me in conformity with your Immaculate Heart.

Let me always trust your Immaculate Heart as a true source of grace and mercy. In sharing in the Passion of your Son, your Immaculate Heart was pierced. May your immaculate love embrace me in moments of suffering.

I beg to make reparation for all offenses against your Immaculate Heart as I offer you my intentions (mention your request).

Amen.

Immaculate Heart of Mary statue that belonged to Mother Angelica (Mother Angelica Tour collection.)

Prayer to the Infant of Prague

Dearest Jesus, tenderly loving us, Your greatest joy is to dwell among us and to bestow Your blessing upon us. Though I am not worthy that You should behold me with love, I feel myself drawn to You, O dear Infant Jesus, because You gladly pardon me and exercise Your almighty power over me.

So many who turned with confidence to You have received graces and had their petitions granted. Behold me, in spirit I kneel before Your miraculous image on Your altar in Prague, and lay open my heart to You, with its prayers, petitions and hopes.

Especially (mention your intentions here)... I enclose in Your loving Heart.

continued

Govern me and do with me and mine according to Your Holy Will, for I know that in Your Divine wisdom and love You will ordain everything for the best.

Almighty and gracious Infant Jesus, do not withdraw Your hand from us, but protect and bless us forever.

I pray You, sweetest Infant, in the name of Your Blessed Mother Mary who cared for You with such tenderness, and by the great reverence with which St. Joseph carried You in his arms, comfort me and make me happy that I may bless and thank You forever with all my heart.

Amen.

The Stations of the Cross
(according to the method of St. Francis of Assisi)

Rita developed a great devotion to the Stations of the Cross. Every day after working at The Timken Company, Rita would ride the bus to St. Anthony Catholic Church to recite the Stations before going home for supper.

1. Pilate condemns Jesus to die
2. Jesus accepts His cross
3. Jesus falls for the first time
4. Jesus meets His mother, Mary
5. Simon of Cyrene helps carry the cross
6. Veronica wipes the face of Jesus
7. Jesus falls for the second time
8. Jesus meets the women of Jerusalem
9. Jesus falls for the third time
10. Jesus is stripped of his clothes
11. Jesus is nailed to the cross
12. Jesus dies on the cross
13. Jesus is taken down from the cross
14. Jesus is placed in the tomb

Preparatory Prayer

Most merciful Lord, with a contrite heart and penitent spirit I bow down before Thy Divine Majesty. I adore Thee as my supreme Lord and Master. I believe in Thee, I hope in Thee, I love Thee above all things. I am heartily sorry for having offended Thee, my only and supreme God. I firmly resolve to amend my life; and although I am unworthy to obtain mercy, yet looking upon Thy Holy Cross I am filled with peace and consolation.

I will, therefore, meditate on Thy sufferings, and visit the Stations in company with Thy sorrowful Mother and my holy Guardian Angel, to promote Thy honor and to save my soul.

I desire to gain all indulgences granted to this holy exercise for myself and for the souls in Purgatory.

O Loving Jesus, inflame my cold heart with Thy love, that I may perform this devotion as perfectly as possible, and that I may live and die in union with Thee.

Amen.

First Station – Jesus Is Condemned to Death

V. We adore Thee, O Christ, and we praise Thee
R. Because by Thy holy Cross, Thou hast redeemed the world.

Jesus, the most innocent of beings, is condemned to death, yes, to the shameful death of the cross. In order to remain a friend of Caesar, Pilate delivers Jesus into the hands of His enemies. O fearful crime, to condemn Innocence to death and to displease God in order to please men.

O innocent Jesus, I have sinned and I am guilty of eternal death; but that I may live, Thou dost gladly accept the unjust sentence of death. For whom then shall I henceforth live if not for Thee, my Lord? If I desire to please men, I can not be Thy servant. Let me, therefore, rather displease the whole world than not please Thee, O Jesus!

Our Father, Hail Mary, Glory be.

V. Lord Jesus, crucified
R. Have mercy on us.

Stations of the Cross, St. Anthony Catholic Church in Canton, Ohio

Second Station – Jesus Carries His Cross

V. We adore Thee, O Christ, and we praise Thee
R. Because by Thy holy Cross, Thou hast redeemed the world.

When our divine Redeemer beheld the Cross, He most willingly reached out to it with His bleeding arms. He embraced it lovingly, kissed it tenderly, took it on His bruised shoulders, and exhausted as He was, carried it joyfully.

O my Jesus, I cannot be Thy friend and follower if I refuse to carry my cross. O beloved cross, I embrace thee, I kiss thee, I joyfully accept Thee from the hand of my God. Far be it from me to glory in anything save in the Cross of my Lord and Redeemer. By it the world shall be crucified to me, and I to the world, that I may be Thine forever.

Our Father, Hail Mary, Glory be.

V. Lord Jesus, crucified
R. Have mercy on us.

Stations of the Cross, St. Anthony Catholic Church in Canton, Ohio

Third Station – Jesus Falls the First Time

V. We adore Thee, O Christ, and we praise Thee
R. Because by Thy holy Cross, Thou hast redeemed the world.

Carrying the Cross, our dear Savior was so weakened with its heavy weight that He fell exhausted to the ground. The Cross was light and sweet to Him, but our sins made it so heavy and hard to carry.

Beloved Jesus, Thou didst carry the burden and the heavy weight of my sins. Should I then not bear in union with Thee my light burden of suffering, and accept the sweet yoke of Thy commandments? Thy yoke is sweet and Thy burden is light. I willingly accept it. I will take up my cross and follow Thee.

Our Father, Hail Mary, Glory be.

V. Lord Jesus, crucified
R. Have mercy on us.

Stations of the Cross, St. Anthony Catholic Church in Canton, Ohio

Fourth Station – Jesus Meets His Blessed Mother

V. We adore Thee, O Christ, and we praise Thee
R. Because by Thy holy Cross, Thou hast redeemed the world.

How sad and how painful must it have been for Mary to behold her beloved Son laden with the Cross, covered with wounds and blood, and driven through the streets by savage executioners! What unspeakable pangs her most tender heart must have experienced! How earnestly did she desire to die instead of Jesus, or at least with Him!

O Jesus, O Mary, I am the cause of the pains that pierced your hearts. Would that my heart might experience some of your sufferings. O Mother, let me share in thy sufferings and those of thy Son, that I may obtain the grace of a happy death.

Our Father, Hail Mary, Glory be.

V. Lord Jesus, crucified
R. Have mercy on us.

Stations of the Cross, St. Anthony Catholic Church in Canton, Ohio

Fifth Station – Simon of Cyrene Helps Jesus Carry His Cross

V. We adore Thee, O Christ, and we praise Thee
R. Because by Thy holy Cross, Thou hast redeemed the world.

Simon of Cyrene was forced to help our exhausted Savior carry His Cross. How pleased would Jesus have been, had Simon offered his services of his own accord. However, Simon was not invited by Christ as you are. He says: "Take up your cross and follow Me." Nevertheless you recoil, and carry it grudgingly.

O Jesus, whosoever does not take up his cross and follow Thee, is not worthy of Thee. Behold, I cheerfully join Thee on the way of the cross. I desire to carry it with all patience until death, that I may prove worthy of Thee.

Our Father, Hail Mary, Glory be.

V. Lord Jesus, crucified
R. Have mercy on us.

Stations of the Cross, St. Anthony Catholic Church in Canton, Ohio

V

Sixth Station – Veronica Wipes the Face of Jesus

V. We adore Thee, O Christ, and we praise Thee
R. Because by Thy holy Cross, Thou hast redeemed the world.

Moved by compassion, Veronica presents her veil to Jesus to wipe His disfigured face. He imprints on it His holy countenance, and returns it to her as a recompense. Shall Christ reward you in like manner? Then you too must do Him a service. But you do a service to Christ every time you perform a work of mercy towards your neighbor; for He says: "What you have done to the least of My brethren, you have done to Me."

Dearest Jesus, what return shall I make Thee for all Thy benefits? Behold, I consecrate myself entirely to Thy service. My whole heart I give to Thee; stamp on it Thy holy image, that I may never forget Thee.

Our Father, Hail Mary, Glory be.

V. Lord Jesus, crucified
R. Have mercy on us.

Stations of the Cross, St. Anthony Catholic Church in Canton, Ohio

VI

Seventh Station – Jesus Falls the Second Time

V. We adore Thee, O Christ, and we praise Thee
R. Because by Thy holy Cross, Thou hast redeemed the world.

Overwhelmed by the weight of the Cross, Jesus falls again to the ground. But the cruel executioners do not permit Him to rest a moment. With thrusts and blows they urge Him onward. With what cruelty Jesus is treated and trampled underfoot! Remember, compassionate soul, that your sins caused Jesus this painful fall.

Have mercy on me, O Jesus, and help me never to fall into my former sins. From this moment I will strive sincerely never to sin again. O Jesus, strengthen me with Thy grace, that I may faithfully carry out my resolution.

Our Father, Hail Mary, Glory be.

V. Lord Jesus, crucified
R. Have mercy on us.

Stations of the Cross, St. Anthony Catholic Church in Canton, Ohio

Eighth Station – Jesus Speaks to the Women of Jerusalem

V. We adore Thee, O Christ, and we praise Thee
R. Because by Thy holy Cross, Thou hast redeemed the world.

Moved by compassion, these devoted women weep over our suffering Savior. But He turns to them and says: "Weep not for Me, but weep for yourselves and your children. Weep for your sins and those of your children; for they are the cause of My suffering." You also must weep over your sins, for there is nothing more pleasing to our Lord and more useful to yourself than the tears you shed out of contrition for your sins.

O Jesus, who shall give my eyes a torrent of tears, that I may day and night weep over my sins? I beseech Thee by Thy bitter and bloody tears to move my heart, so that tears may flow in abundance from my eyes, and that I may weep over Thy sufferings and over my sins until death.

Our Father, Hail Mary, Glory be.

V. Lord Jesus, crucified
R. Have mercy on us.

Stations of the Cross, St. Anthony Catholic Church in Canton, Ohio

Ninth Station – Jesus Falls the Third Time

V. We adore Thee, O Christ, and we praise Thee
R. Because by Thy holy Cross, Thou hast redeemed the world.

Exhausted at the foot of Calvary, Jesus falls for the third time to the ground. How painful it must have been to reopen all the wounds of His tender body by these repeated falls. And how enormous must my sins be, to cause Jesus to fall so painfully. Had not Jesus taken my sins upon Himself, they would have plunged me into the abyss of Hell.

Most merciful Jesus, I return Thee a thousand thanks for not permitting me to die in my sins and fall into the abyss of Hell, as I have deserved so often. Enkindle in me a sincere desire to amend my life. Let me never again fall into sin, but grant me the grace of final perseverance.

Our Father, Hail Mary, Glory be.

V. Lord Jesus, crucified
R. Have mercy on us.

Stations of the Cross, St. Anthony Catholic Church in Canton, Ohio

Tenth Station – Jesus Is Stripped of His Garments

V. We adore Thee, O Christ, and we praise Thee
R. Because by Thy holy Cross, Thou hast redeemed the world.

Arriving on Calvary, Jesus was cruelly deprived of His garments. How painful the stripping must have been because the garments adhered to His mangled body, so that in removing them His flesh was torn away. Jesus' garments are taken so that He may die possessed of nothing. How happy shall I die after laying aside my evil habits and tendencies!

Help me, O Jesus, to amend my life. Let it be renewed according to Thy will and desire. However painful the correction may be to me, I will not spare myself. With the assistance of Thy grace, I will refrain from all sinful pleasure and vain amusement, that I may die happy and live forever.

Our Father, Hail Mary, Glory be.

V. Lord Jesus, crucified
R. Have mercy on us.

Stations of the Cross, St. Anthony Catholic Church in Canton, Ohio

Eleventh Station – Jesus Is Nailed to the Cross

V. We adore Thee, O Christ, and we praise Thee
R. Because by Thy holy Cross, Thou hast redeemed the world.

Stripped of His garments, Jesus is violently thrown down on the Cross. His hands and His feet are nailed to it in the most cruel way. Jesus remains silent because it so pleases His heavenly Father. He suffers patiently because He suffers for you. How do you act in sufferings and trials? How fretful and impatient, how full of complaints are you!

O Jesus, meek and patient Lamb, I renounce forever my impatience. Crucify, O Lord, my flesh, with its evil desires and vices. Punish and afflict me in this life, but spare me in the next. I resign myself altogether to Thy holy will. May it be done in all things.

Our Father, Hail Mary, Glory be.

V. Lord Jesus, crucified
R. Have mercy on us.

Twelfth Station – Jesus Dies on the Cross

V. We adore Thee, O Christ, and we praise Thee
R. Because by Thy holy Cross, Thou hast redeemed the world.

Behold Jesus crucified! Behold His wounds received for love of you! His whole appearance betokens love. His head is bent to kiss you. His arms are extended to embrace you. His heart is open to receive you. Oh what love! Jesus dies on the Cross, to preserve you from eternal death.

Most lovable Jesus, grant that I may die for love of Thee. I will endeavor to die to the world and its vanities when I behold Thee on the Cross covered with wounds and crowned with thorns. Merciful Jesus, take me into Thy wounded heart, that I may despise all perishable things, to live and die for Thee alone.

Our Father, Hail Mary, Glory be.

V. Lord Jesus, crucified
R. Have mercy on us.

Stations of the Cross, St. Anthony Catholic Church in Canton, Ohio

Thirteenth Station – Jesus Is Taken Down From the Cross

V. We adore Thee, O Christ, and we praise Thee
R. Because by Thy holy Cross, Thou hast redeemed the world.

Jesus did not descend from the Cross, but remained on it till His death. When taken down, He rested on the bosom of His beloved Mother as He had so often done in life. Persevere in your good resolutions, and do not flee from the cross. For he who perseveres till the end shall be saved. Consider, moreover, how pure the heart should be that receives the body and blood of Jesus Christ in the adorable Sacrament of the Altar.

O Lord Jesus crucified! I most earnestly entreat Thee: Help me do what is right and let me not be separated from Thy Cross, for on it I desire to live and to die. Create in me, O Lord, a clean heart, that I may worthily receive Thee in Holy Communion, and that Thou may remain in me, and I in Thee for all eternity.

Our Father, Hail Mary, Glory be.

V. Lord Jesus, crucified
R. Have mercy on us.

Stations of the Cross, St. Anthony Catholic Church in Canton, Ohio

Fourteenth Station – Jesus Is Laid in the Tomb

V. We adore Thee, O Christ, and we praise Thee
R. Because by Thy holy Cross, Thou hast redeemed the world.

The body of Jesus is laid in a stranger's tomb. He Who in this world had not whereon to rest His head, would have no grave of His own after death. You whose heart is still attached to this world, despise it that you may not perish with it.

O Jesus, Thou hast singled me out from the world; what then shall I seek in it? Thou hast created me for Heaven; what then shall I desire upon earth? Depart from me, deceitful world, with thy vanities! Henceforth I will walk the way of the Cross traced out for me by my Redeemer, and journey onward to my heavenly home where my rest and my joy shall be forever.

Our Father, Hail Mary, Glory be.

V. Lord Jesus, crucified
R. Have mercy on us.

Stations of the Cross, St. Anthony Catholic Church in Canton, Ohio

When Rita was baptized on September 19, 1923, at St. Anthony Catholic Church, her mother, Mae, after the ceremony, took her baby daughter, placed her before Our Lady of Sorrows and said "I give you my daughter." This event was truly significant.

One autumn afternoon, twenty years later, in 1943 as Rita prayed before that same statue, she was deeply touched by an experience of God that encouraged her to give her life to Jesus.

Sorrowful Mother statue, St. Anthony Catholic Church in Canton, Ohio

Sorrowful Mother Prayer - Stabat Mater

At the cross her station keeping, Stood the mournful Mother weeping, Close to Jesus to the last.

Through her heart, His sorrow sharing, All His bitter anguish bearing, Now at length the sword had passed.

Oh, how sad and sore distressed Was that Mother highly blest, Of the sole begotten One!

Christ above in torment hangs. She beneath beholds the pangs Of her dying glorious Son.

Is there one who would not weep, Whelmed in miseries so deep, Christ's dear Mother to behold?

Can the human heart refrain From partaking in her pain, In that Mother's pain untold?

Bruised, derided, cursed, defiled, She beheld her tender Child, All with bloody scourges rent.

For the sins of His own nation, Saw Him hang in desolation Till His spirit forth He sent. *continued*

O thou Mother, fount of love! Touch my spirit from above, Make my heart with thine accord.

Make me feel as thou hast felt; Make my soul to glow and melt With the love of Christ my Lord.

Holy Mother, pierce me through; In my heart each wound renew Of my Savior crucified.

Let me share with thee His pain, Who for all my sins was slain, Who for me in torment died.

Let me mingle tears with thee, Mourning Him who mourned for me, All the days that I may live.

By the Cross with thee to stay; There with thee to weep and pray, Is all I ask of thee to give.

Virgin of all virgins best, Listen to my fond request: Let me share thy grief divine.

Let me to my last breath, In my body bear the death Of that dying Son of thine. *continued*

Wounded with His every wound, Steep my soul till it hath swooned In His very blood away.

Be to me, O Virgin, nigh, Lest in flames I burn and die, In His awful Judgment Day.

Christ, when Thou shalt call me hence, Be Thy Mother my defense, Be Thy Cross my victory.

While my body here decays, May my soul Thy goodness praise, Safe in Paradise with Thee.

Amen.

Sorrowful Mother statue, St. Anthony Catholic Church in Canton, Ohio

In August 1944, Rita gave her life to Jesus as a "bride of Christ." She joined the Poor Clares of Perpetual Adoration, a Franciscan Order dedicated to praying before the Blessed Sacrament.

St. Francis Peace Prayer

Lord, make me an instrument of Your peace: where there is hatred, let me sow love; where there is injury, pardon; where there is doubt, faith; where there is despair, hope; where there is darkness, light; where there is sadness, joy.

O Divine Master, grant that I may not so much seek to be consoled as to console; to be understood as to understand; to be loved as to love. For it is in giving that we receive; it is in pardoning that we are pardoned; and it is in dying that we are born to eternal life.

Amen.

St. Francis statue, Sancta Clara Monastery in Canton, Ohio

St. Clare Prayer

God of Mercy, You inspired Saint Clare
with the love of poverty. By the help of her prayers may
we follow Christ in poverty of spirit and come to the
joyful vision of Your glory in the kingdom of Heaven.

We ask this through our Lord Jesus Christ, Your Son, Who
lives and reigns with You and the Holy Spirit, one God,
forever and ever.

Amen.

Blessing of Saint Clare

May Almighty God bless you; May He look upon you with
the eyes of His Mercy and give you His peace.

Here below may He pour forth His graces on you
abundantly and in heaven may He place you among His
saints.

St. Clare statue, Sancta Clara
Monastery in Canton, Ohio

St. Clare's Prayer Before the Crucifix

I behold the Lord.
I see His outstretched hands.
I see the blood from His wounds.
I see the love in the eyes of Jesus.
I see His gracious acceptance of me.

Jesus has come out of the tomb –
He still has the scars, but now they are glorious, with the glory of heaven.
Still looking at the Lord, I reach out and touch Him.
I hold the Lord – and I am held in His love.

Love enfolds.
It is no longer I that live, but Christ that lives in me.
I am secure in the Lord.
I can look out, now, through the Lord's eyes.
I can see the world as He created it, in His mercy.
I can see my sisters and brothers with His love,
and I can worship the Father through the eyes of the Son in the Love of the Holy Spirit.

San Damiano Cross
(public domain)

The Poor Clares of Perpetual Adoration pray the Divine Office as a community. Sister Angelica said these prayers with her fellow Sisters every day of her religious life.

Canticle of Zechariah

(Morning: Benedictus)

Blessed be the Lord, the God of Israel; He has come to His people and set them free. He has raised up for us a mighty Savior, born of the house of His servant David. Through His holy prophets He promised of old that He would save us from our enemies, from the hands of all who hate us. He promised to show mercy to our fathers and to remember His holy covenant.

This was the oath He swore to our father Abraham: to set us free from the hands of our enemies, free to worship Him without fear, holy and righteous in His sight all the days of our life. You, my child, shall be called the prophet of the Most High; for you will go before the Lord to prepare His way, to give His people knowledge of salvation by the forgiveness of their sins.

In the tender compassion of our God, the dawn from on high shall break upon us, to shine on those who dwell in darkness and the shadow of death, and to guide our feet into the way of peace.

Canticle of Mary
(Evening: Magnificat)

My soul proclaims the greatness of the Lord,
My Spirit rejoices in God my Saviour
For He has looked with favour on His lowly servant.

From this day all generations will call me blessed:
The Almighty has done great things for me,
And holy is His Name.

He has mercy on those who fear Him
In every generation.

He has shown the strength of His arm,
He has scattered the proud in their conceit.

He has cast down the mighty from their thrones,
And has lifted up the lowly.

He has filled the hungry with good things,
And the rich He has sent away empty.

He has come to the help of His servant Israel
For He has remembered His promise of mercy,
The promise He made to our fathers,
To Abraham and his children forever.

Gospel Canticle of Simeon
(Night prayer)

Lord, now let Your servant go in peace; Your word has been fulfilled, my own eyes have seen the salvation which You have prepared in the sight of the people; a light to reveal You to the nations and the glory of Your people Israel.

Protect us, Lord as we stay awake, watch over us as we sleep, that awake we may keep watch with Christ and asleep rest in His peace.

Hail Holy Queen
(Concluding night prayer)

Hail, holy Queen, Mother of mercy, our life, our sweetness and our hope.

To thee do we cry, poor banished children of Eve; to thee do we send up our sighs, mourning and weeping in this valley of tears.

Turn then, most gracious advocate, thine eyes of mercy toward us, and after this our exile show unto us the blessed fruit of thy womb, Jesus. O clement, O loving, O sweet Virgin Mary!

Amen.

Mary, Ark of the Covenant window,
St. Raphael Center in Canton, Ohio

Te Deum
(Sunday and feast day prayer)

You are God, we praise You.
You are the Lord; we acclaim You.
You are the eternal Father.
All creation worships You.

To You all angels, all the powers of heaven,
Cherubim and Seraphim, sing in endless praise:
Holy, Holy, Holy Lord, God of power and might,
heaven and earth are full of Your glory.

The glorious company of apostles praise You.
The noble fellowship of prophets praise You.
The white-robed army of martyrs praise You.

Throughout the world the holy Church acclaims You;
Father of majesty unbounded, Your true and only Son,
worthy of all worship, and the Holy Spirit, advocate and
guide. *continued*

You, Christ, are the king of glory, the eternal Son of the Father. When You became man to set us free, You did not shun the Virgin's womb.

You overcame the sting of death and opened the kingdom of heaven to all believers. You are seated at God's right hand in glory. We believe that You will come and be our judge.

Come then, Lord, and help Your people, bought with the price of Your own blood, and bring us with Your saints to glory everlasting.

V. Save Your people, Lord, and bless Your inheritance.
R. Govern and uphold them now and always.

V. Day by day we bless You.
R. We praise Your name forever.

V. Keep us today, Lord, from all sin.
R. Have mercy on us, Lord, have mercy.

V. Lord, show us Your love and mercy,
R. For we have put our trust in You.

V. In You, Lord, is our hope;
R. Let us never be put to shame.

The Poor Clares of Perpetual Adoration recite the Rosary together in their chapel every day.

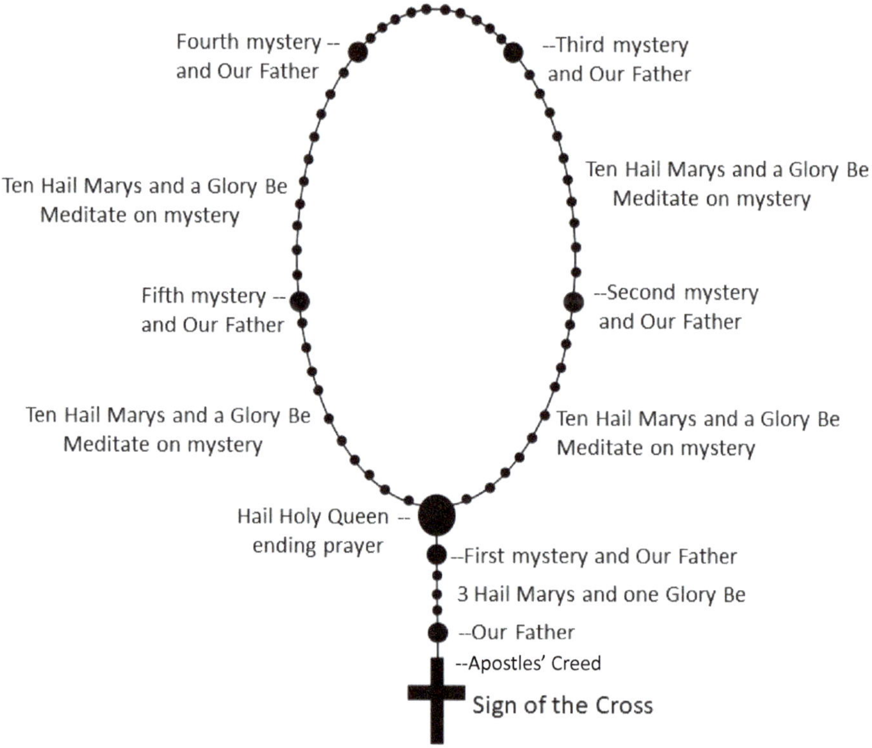

- Fourth mystery -- and Our Father
- Third mystery -- and Our Father
- Ten Hail Marys and a Glory Be / Meditate on mystery
- Ten Hail Marys and a Glory Be / Meditate on mystery
- Fifth mystery -- and Our Father
- Second mystery -- and Our Father
- Ten Hail Marys and a Glory Be / Meditate on mystery
- Ten Hail Marys and a Glory Be / Meditate on mystery
- Hail Holy Queen -- ending prayer
- First mystery and Our Father
- 3 Hail Marys and one Glory Be
- Our Father
- Apostles' Creed
- Sign of the Cross

"*If I had an army to say the Rosary, I could conquer the world.*"

-Blessed Pope Pius IX

The Rosary

Joyful Mysteries of the Rosary
Monday and Saturday
1. The Annunciation of the Lord to Mary
2. The Visitation of Mary to Elizabeth
3. The Nativity of our Lord Jesus Christ
4. The Presentation of our Lord
5. Finding Jesus in the Temple at age twelve

Sorrowful Mysteries of the Rosary
Tuesday and Friday
1. The Agony of Jesus in the Garden
2. The Scourging at the Pillar
3. Jesus is Crowned with Thorns
4. Jesus Carries the Cross
5. The Crucifixion of our Lord

Glorious Mysteries of the Rosary
Wednesday and Sunday
1. The Resurrection of Jesus Christ
2. The Ascension of Jesus into Heaven
3. The Descent of the Holy Spirit
4. The Assumption of Mary into Heaven
5. Mary is Crowned as Queen of Heaven and Earth

Luminous Mysteries of the Rosary
Thursday
1. The Baptism in the Jordan River
2. The Wedding at Cana
3. The Proclamation of the Kingdom
4. The Transfiguration
5. The Institution of the Eucharist

Jesus in the Blessed Sacrament is the heart of the Poor Clare Community. Sister Angelica spent at least one hour of adoration before the Blessed Sacrament every day.

Prayers before the Blessed Sacrament

Anima Christi

Soul of Christ, sanctify me.
Body of Christ, save me.
Blood of Christ, inebriate me.
Water from the side of Christ, wash me.
Passion of Christ, strengthen me.
O Good Jesus, hear me.
Within Thy wounds hide me.
Suffer me not to be separated from Thee.
From the malignant enemy defend me.
In the hour of my death call me
And bid me come unto Thee,
That with all Thy saints,
I may praise Thee
Forever and ever.

Amen.

Monstrance at Sancta Clara Monastery in Canton, Ohio

Divine Praises

Blessed be God.
Blessed be His Holy Name.
Blessed be Jesus Christ, true God and true Man.
Blessed be the Name of Jesus.
Blessed be His Most Sacred Heart.
Blessed be His Most Precious Blood.
Blessed be Jesus in the Most Holy Sacrament of the Altar.
Blessed be the Holy Spirit, the Paraclete.
Blessed be the Great Mother of God, Mary most Holy.
Blessed be her Holy and Immaculate Conception.
Blessed be her Glorious Assumption.
Blessed be the name of Mary, Virgin and Mother.
Blessed be St. Joseph, her most chaste spouse.
Blessed be God in His Angels and in His Saints.

May the heart of Jesus, in the Most Blessed Sacrament, be praised, adored and loved with grateful affection, at every moment, in all the tabernacles of the world, even to the end of time.

Amen.

O Saving Victim

O saving Victim, opening wide
The gate of heaven to man below!
Our foes press on from every side;
Thine aid supply, Thy strength bestow.
To Thy great name be endless praise,
Immortal Godhead, One in Three;
Oh, grant us endless length of days,
In our true native land with Thee.

Amen.

O Salutaris

O salutaris Hostia, Quae caeli pandis ostium:
Bella premunt hostilia, Da robur fer auxilium.
Uni trinoque Domino, Sit sempiterna gloria:
Qui vitam sine termino, Nobis donet in patria.

Amen.

Down in Adoration Falling

Down in adoration falling, Lo! the Sacred Host we hail. Lo! o'er ancient forms departing, Newer rites of grace prevail. Faith for all defects supplying, Where the feeble senses fail. To the everlasting Father, And the Son Who reigns on high With the Holy Spirit proceeding, Forth from Each eternally, Be salvation, honor, blessing, Might and endless majesty.

Amen.

Tantum Ergo

Tantum ergo Sacramentum, Veneremur cernui:
Et antiquum documentum, Novo cedat ritui:
Praestet fides supplementum, Sensuum defectui.
Genitori, Genitoque, Laus et jubilatio,
Salus, honor, virtus quoque, Sit et benedictio:
Procedenti ab utroque, Compar sit laudatio.

Amen.

Prayer of St. Alphonsus Liguori
(Visit to the Blessed Sacrament)

My Lord Jesus Christ, Who because of Your love for men remain night and day in the Blessed Sacrament, full of pity and of love, awaiting, calling and welcoming all who come to visit You, I believe that You are present here on the altar. I adore You, and I thank You for all the graces You have bestowed on me, especially for having given me Yourself in this Sacrament, for having given me Your most holy Mother Mary to plead for me, and for having called me to visit You in this church.

I now salute Your most loving Heart, and that for three ends: first, in thanksgiving for this great gift; secondly, to make amends to You for all the outrages committed against You in this Sacrament by Your enemies; thirdly, I intend by this visit to adore You in all the places on earth in which You are present in the Blessed Sacrament and in which You are least honored and most abandoned.
continued

My Jesus, I love You with my whole heart. I am very sorry for having so many times offended Your infinite goodness. With the help of Your grace, I promise never to offend You again. And now, unworthy though I am, I consecrate myself to You without reserve. I renounce and give entirely to You my will, my affection, my desires and all that I possess. For the future, dispose of me and all I have as You please.

All I ask of You is Your holy love, final perseverance and that I may carry out Your will perfectly. I recommend to You the souls in Purgatory, especially those who had the greatest devotion to the Blessed Sacrament and to the Blessed Virgin Mary. I also recommend to You all poor sinners.

Finally, my dear Saviour, I unite all my desires with the desires of Your most loving Heart; and I offer them, thus united, to the Eternal Father, and beseech Him, in Your name and for love of You, to accept and grant them.

Amen.

Angel of Peace Prayer
(Fatima, Spring 1916)

My God, I believe, I adore, I hope, and I love You! I beg pardon for those who do not believe, do not adore, do not hope and do not love You.

Angel of Peace Prayer
(Fatima, Autumn 1916)

O Most Holy Trinity, Father, Son and Holy Spirit, I adore Thee profoundly.

I offer Thee the most precious Body, Blood, Soul and Divinity of Jesus Christ, present in all the tabernacles of the world, in reparation for the outrages, sacrileges and indifference by which He is offended.

By the infinite merits of the Sacred Heart of Jesus and the Immaculate Heart of Mary, I beg the conversion of poor sinners.

Sister Angelica spent 17 years at the Poor Clare Monastery in Canton, Ohio. She began a new foundation of Poor Clares in Birmingham, Alabama, in 1962. Henceforth she was known as Mother Angelica.

Daily Schedule of the Poor Clares of Perpetual Adoration

The rhythm of our day arises from our healthy balance of prayer, study, work, silence and relationship. This climate promotes growth and maturity that is fully human, Christian and Franciscan. It leads to a gradual transformation of our lives into the image and likeness of God.

6:00 a.m.
Meditation

6:30 a.m.
Morning Prayer
Breakfast
Spiritual Reading /
Exercise

9:00 a.m.
The Holy Sacrifice of Mass; followed by Mid-morning; Prayer, Prayer of Thanksgiving (personal)

10:15 a.m.
Work

12:00 p.m.
Dinner with Table Readings or in Silence; Recreation follows after dishes for Novitiate sisters

1:30 p.m. - 3:00 p.m.
Personal Time

3:00 p.m. - 4:00 p.m.
Formation Study
Work

4:45 p.m.
Mid-Afternoon Prayer
Evening Prayer
Communal Rosary

6:00 p.m.
Supper

6:00 p.m. - 7:00 p.m.
Holy Hour (Every Friday)

6:45 p.m.
Recreation

7:30 p.m.
Night Prayer

8:00 p.m.
Grand Silence

Find out more at www.poorclares.org

Litany of Humility
(Favorite prayer of Mother Angelica)

O Jesus! Meek and humble of heart, hear me.

From the desire of being esteemed, deliver me Jesus.

From the desire of being loved, deliver me Jesus.

From the desire of being extolled, deliver me Jesus.

From the desire of being honored, deliver me Jesus.

From the desire of being praised, deliver me Jesus.

From the desire of being preferred, deliver me Jesus.

From the desire of being consulted, deliver me Jesus.

From the desire of being approved, deliver me Jesus.

From the fear of being humiliated, deliver me Jesus.

From the fear of being despised, deliver me Jesus.

From the fear of suffering rebukes, deliver me Jesus.

From the fear of being calumniated, deliver me Jesus.

From the fear of being forgotten, deliver me Jesus.

From the fear of being ridiculed, deliver me Jesus.

From the fear of being wronged, deliver me Jesus.

From the fear of being suspected, deliver me Jesus.

continued

That others may be loved more than I, Jesus, grant me the grace to desire it.

That others may be esteemed more than I, Jesus, grant me the grace to desire it.

That in the opinion of the world, others may increase and I may decrease, Jesus, grant me the grace to desire it.

That others may be chosen and I set aside, Jesus, grant me the grace to desire it.

That others may be praised and I unnoticed, Jesus, grant me the grace to desire it.

That others may be preferred to me in everything, Jesus, grant me the grace to desire it.

That others become holier than I, provided that I may become as holy as I should, Jesus, grant me the grace to desire it.

Prayer Before the Blessed Sacrament by Pope St. John XXIII

O Jesus, present in the Sacrament of the altar, teach all the nations to serve You with willing hearts, knowing that to serve God is to reign.

May Your sacrament, O Jesus, be light to the mind, strength to the will, joy to the heart. May it be the support of the weak, the comfort of the suffering, the wayfaring bread of salvation for the dying and for all the pledge of future glory.

Desire For Closer Union
(St. Bonaventure)

Lord Jesus Christ, pierce my soul with Your love so that I may always long for You alone, Who are the bread of angels and the fulfillment of the soul's deepest desires. May my heart always hunger and feed upon You so that my soul may be filled with the sweetness of Your presence.

May my soul thirst for You, Who are the source of life, wisdom, knowledge, light and all the riches of God our Father. May I always seek and find You, think upon You, speak to you and do all things for honor and glory of Your holy name. Be always my only hope, my peace, my refuge and my help in whom my heart is rooted so that I may never be separated from You.

Amen.

In 1995, Mother Angelica visited Columbia during a tour of South America and had a mystical experience with the "Divino Niño," that is, the Divine Child Jesus. She developed a great devotion to Him, so much so that she built a church in His honor.

Prayer to the Divino Niño in Difficult Times

Divine Child Jesus,
In my difficulties: help me
From the enemies of my soul: save me
In my errors: enlighten me
In my doubts and pains: comfort me
In my solitudes: be with me
In my diseases: invigorate me
When others despise me: encourage me
In temptations: defend me
In difficult hours: strengthen me
With Your paternal heart: love me
With your immense power: protect me
And, into Your arms, when I die: receive me.

Amen.

Detail of the Christ Child from the Madonna Delle Ombre by Fra Angelico

Prayer to the Nine Choirs of Angels

O Holy Angels, watch over us at all times during this perilous life;

O Holy Archangels, be our guides on the way to heaven;

O Heavenly choir of the Principalities, govern us in soul and body;

O Mighty Powers, preserve us against the wiles of the demons;

O Celestial Virtues, give us strength and courage in the battle of life;

O Powerful Dominions, obtain for us authority over the rebellion of our flesh;

O Sacred Thrones, grant us peace with God and man;

O Brilliant Cherubim, illuminate our minds with heavenly knowledge;

O Burning Seraphim, enkindle in our hearts the fire of charity.

Amen.

The Assumption of the Virgin, by Francesco Botticini

Mother Angelica died at Our Lady of the Angels Monastery in Hanceville, Alabama, on March 27, 2016. It was Easter Sunday.

Prayers for the Dead

God our Father,
Your power brings us to birth,
Your providence guides our lives,
and by Your command we return to dust.

Lord, those who die still live in Your presence,
their lives change but do not end.
I pray in hope for my family,
relatives and friends,
and for all the dead known to You alone.

In company with Christ,
Who died and now lives,
may they rejoice in Your kingdom,
where all our tears are wiped away.
Unite us together again in one family,
to sing Your praise forever and ever.

Amen.

Stained glass window, St. Peter Catholic Church in Canton, Ohio

Eternal Rest Prayer

Eternal rest grant unto her, O Lord. And let perpetual light shine upon her.

May she rest in peace.

May her soul and souls of all the faithful departed through the mercy of God, rest in peace.

Amen.

De Profundis - Psalm 130

Out of the depths I cry to You, O Lord,
Lord, hear my voice! O let Your ears be attentive
to the voice of my pleading. If You, O Lord,
should mark our guilt, Lord, who would survive?
But with You is found forgiveness; for this we
revere You.

My soul is waiting for the Lord. I count on His
word. My soul is longing for the Lord more than
the watchman for daybreak.

Let the watchman count on daybreak and Israel on
the Lord.

Because with the Lord there is mercy and fullness
of redemption, Israel indeed He will redeem from
all its iniquity.

Glory be to the Father...

About Us

This prayer book was compiled by Barbara A. Gaskell. She is the founder and director of St. Raphael Center, Inc. in Canton, Ohio. St. Raphael Center, Inc. is a not-for-profit Catholic evangelization center that houses; St. Raphael Books & Gifts, studios of the Living Bread Radio Network, Mary, Ark of the Covenant Chapel, Visitation Room, outdoor Rosary Garden with Lourdes Grotto, and a memorial to the unborn.

St. Raphael Center, Inc. also became the official distributor of DS Music Productions, in 2019, which produces the music of world-renowned singer DANA. In 2015, Barbara launched the Mother Angelica Tour which focuses on the early life of Rita Rizzo. Learn more about the tour and the Catholic campus in Canton by visiting StRaphaelCenter.com.

St. Raphael Books & Gifts
and CatholicBook.net

MotherAngelicaTour.com

Reflections. . .

www.ingramcontent.com/pod-product-compliance
Lightning Source LLC
Chambersburg PA
CBHW041228070526
44584CB00006B/327